THE NEXT
COUNTRY

THE NEXT COUNTRY

IDRA NOVEY

ALICE JAMES BOOKS
FARMINGTON, MAINE

10 9 8 7 6 5 4 3 2 1

Alice James Books are published by Alice James Poetry Cooperative, Inc.,
an affiliate of the University of Maine at Farmington.

ALICE JAMES BOOKS
238 MAIN STREET
FARMINGTON, ME 04938

www.alicejamesbooks.org

Library of Congress Cataloging-in-Publication Data

Novey, Idra, 1978-
  The next country / by Idra Novey.
    p. cm.
  Includes bibliographical references.
  ISBN 978-1-882295-71-5
  I. Title.

  PS3614.O928N49 2008
  811'.6–dc22

                        2008030879

Alice James Books gratefully acknowledges support from the University
of Maine at Farmington and the National Endowment for the Arts. ❧

COVER ART: Matthew Cusick, "Course of Empire (Mixmaster II)"
2006, mixed media on wood panel
48 inches x 77 inches
Courtesy of the artist

CONTENTS

Aubade for Viña del Mar

I

II

III

IV

ACKNOWLEDGMENTS

A selection of these poems appeared in a chapbook chosen by Carolyn Forché for a Poetry Society of America Chapbook Fellowship and published by the PSA in 2005. Some of the poems also appeared in the following publications, sometimes in earlier versions:

AGNI: "Into the Atacama"
Barrow Street: "Aubade for Viña del Mar"
Chattahoochee Review: "Property"
Court Green: "Pausing Outside a House"
LIT: "Trans" and "Highway Town"
Paris Review: "The Experiment"
Pequod: "Customs"
Ploughshares: "Maddox Road"
Subtropics: "A History in Six Couplets"
Slate: "Stranger"
Small Spiral Notebook: "Tikal," "Postcard of Two Birds, Scattered Feathers," and "To Byzantium, by Train"
Third Rail: The Poetry of Rock and Roll: "The Wailers in Estadio Nacional"
Verse Daily: "Aubade for Viña del Mar"
Washington Square: "A Maça No Oscuro"

Many thanks to the editors of the publications listed above and to the Poetry Society of America, the Dorothy Sargent Rosenberg Fund, and the Millay Colony for the Arts, where a number of these poems were completed.

Great heaps of thanks also go to the following poets and friends for their careful reading and encouragement: K. D. Henley, Aimee Walker, Becka McKay, Jennifer Kronovet, Ram Devineni, Joseph Legaspi, Katherine Cortes, Kythe Heller, Peter Waldor and the whole AJB Board and staff, headed by the intrepid April Ossmann and Lacy Simons.

This book is dedicated to my parents, as far apart in their lives as they may be now, and to the many family members and friends who supported the making of these poems, especially my stupendous sister Becca.

And as always, to Leo Novik, *mi pareja espectácular*, whose love makes me joyful.

It is the history of the idea of war
that is beneath our other histories.

—Muriel Rukeyser

AUBADE FOR VIÑA DEL MAR

I follow a stray dog
so he'll stop following me
and a violin begins forming
in the pocket of my coat.

I have no ear for tuning
but it is six A.M.
and I will soon be the owner
of a complete instrument.

Now it's almost seven o'clock
and a torso of wood
is pressing into my side.
In the other pocket, the poke
of a bow.

EAST OF HERE

In the next country over, the lotus
is chocolate-brown and grows tall

as maize. The sole religion seems
to be bread, any kind, including

one similar to rye, but made of lotus.
And if someone you've doted on

dies there defending
the nation, seven emissaries

for the president come by,
all wearing stethoscopes,

and listen to your heart. Afterward,
they offer artichoke sandwiches

in official blue Saran Wrap and hand you
a list of either answers

or questions, but never both.
There's a road if you want to go.

CUSTOMS

Passports, please

    Skimming facts, stamps,
    the land disappearing
    beneath the Pacific's salty foam.

        A thought of the wet stones
        I placed once
                at each corner of our tent,

           afraid the wind might wheel us off—

And the purpose of your travel

    Claret flowers in the desert, sir,
    and the dunes, of course,
             their muted shifting being
             the real history
                   of loyalties:

             two people in a line, one suitcase
             between them,

      though only you
      are a citizen here—

             and I pocket my fear:
             sooner or later,
             you'll return to this coast of yours

without me.

Carrying anything with you today
anything perishable
                    fruits
                         plants

   Your warm hand in my pocket
   in search of secrets,
                    your credo:

            we are what we carry undeclared.

STRANGER

Person not a member
of a group. A visitor,
guest, or the breast
that brushes your arm
on the subway. Person
with whom you've had
no acquaintance but who's taken
your rocking chair
from the curbside
and curls up in it
and closes her eyes.
Person in line
behind you now, waiting
for a glass of water,
of whiskey, or elixir.
Person logging online
at the same second
from the Home Depot in Lima
or in search of the Dalai Lama.
Person not privy or party
to a decision, edict, etcetera,
but who's eaten
from the same fork
at the pizzeria
and kissed your wilder sister
on New Year's. Person assigned
to feed the tiger at the zoo
where you slipped your hand

                              once

into the palm
of somebody else's father.

SCENES FROM MOVING VEHICLES, I

Dark-haired and given to staring,
the border guards mistook her

for an immigrant, sneaking in
with this swell American family, all belted

into their sweltering Chevy.
Her? Oh, she's been following us

for years, the father joked
and carried on, relentless, for miles

into Texas. The girl, clement and ready
for elsewhere, decided she was meant

to unbuckle and exit alone.
To escape. And be mistaken.

THE WAILERS IN ESTADIO NACIONAL

Before the concert, Ziggy Marley
says it again: *for the detained,
once tortured in this stadium—we play
for you.*
      Two bare-chested boys
lift their joints and shout the name
of an uncle. From where I lie on a blanket,
everyone standing looks tall, hands
easy in their pockets—
                 no way to tell
who was conceived under curfew
and who in exile, returned now
from East Berlin.
           The oval sky
above the stadium dims, dusky—
the cut purple of Santiago smog
and summer, of plums.
            Ziggy says
the first song's about democracy—
the lyrics in English, message
turned to cadence, to the grind and slip
of hips along the pocked wall, wheels
of the slow machine
               that is a country.

A HISTORY IN SIX COUPLETS

Called a bird, the distant
dying city died as a bird does.

Dogs circled it, gray mud
caked on their haunches.

And all around,
a kind of tilting.

All around, chunks of concrete
like torn bread.

When asked about hunger,
the children replied with hunger.

When asked about birds,
they opened their mouths to the sky.

FOR MY SISTER, DRIVING AWAY

From a picture, no one guesses
the relation till I explain

about our fathers: one black
and one white. Then everyone finds

a resemblance: your cheekbones,
they say. No, it's your jawline.

Or maybe the eyebrows.
When I think *story*, I start

with the mother, but maybe
I've been telling it backward.

     •

Where the water streamed
swiftest over the rocks, our mother

rolled up her pants, waded in.
Swaying, bell-like, almost willing

her fall, she called for us
and we laughed at her.

For hours after, that river
kept delivering itself between us.

Is it possible to have a mother
pitching toward the water,

and alongside that falling
a margin of happiness?

●

Outside a Cineplex, I spotted a woman
in an ill-fitting dress. She was in line,

but only half-so. People milled
around her, her face like a town

along the Hudson—a mix of prison
and wilderness. I wondered

if she had children, if when they spoke
it was like unstitching

that ill-fitting dress
covering her body, if even then

their talk was a whisper, a sort of scissor
scraping the skin.

ABOUT A ROAD

near the Panama Canal, 2004

The driver says he knows it,
the one out to the zoo, the old winding

highway for Americans,
or whoever would serve them.

The one past the last lock
to the Pacific, he says. All that water

lifting and lowering like the back
of a nurse. But what is it

you're looking for, he asks, and I tell him
the little garden inside the zoo,

the botanical garden, and of course
the tigers. They died, he says.

There's a blind donkey in the cage now.
People watch it just the same.

THE EXPERIMENT

We all sensed we were in it, but didn't know why.
I suspected it was about ethics, but each week
seemed as much a test in coping—the artistry
of partial views.
                    But if so, who'd been scripted
as the control group? Was it us, wilting
for all to see in the humid city, so many tulips
crushed into a pewter vase—
                              or was it others,
in the suburbs, who kept to their cars and tended
to despair apart, in private, where no one
would suspect them of sorrow until they'd already
moved on?
          The study continues: the keeping
of museums, of dictionaries with our best words.
A wild faith that someone will want to see
what we have made.

PROPERTY

Domain

My mother wants
a horse ranch, mornings
of mares. Enough land
to disappear on
and still know the gullies.

And seasons, she says,
will only happen
in the evenings. Midday
will always yield sun,
warming the walnut stools

where my sisters and I
will linger,
we who never eat
in her kitchen all at once.

Forget the linen lost
in her last eviction.
When my mother wishes,
it is for open miles.

And should it snow, come
evening, we'll just wait
for it to blanket the fields,
and harness a sorrel
to her red sleigh.

The Vehicle

Sunday after soccer, Marcelo tells me
he was one of three to survive

his border crossing. Seven
did not. How, running to hide

in a junkyard, he heard their bodies
drop behind him. Eventually, he says,

he'll drive back to Montenegro
in a silver Lexus, a doctor

of something, and stir up
the yellow dust on his brother's road.

The Record

From his bedroom,
Neruda saw a painted board

wash ashore, chipped
and blue, soggy from the sea.

There it is, he shouted,
my desk, come to me at last,

and swiftly mounted it
on these bricks, wrote

upon its azure back
a thousand verses

until he had nothing left to say,
and cursed it.

TRANS

-late

To speak of origins requires mastery
of the verb *to be*. I used to be, for example,
a little unwieldy. What an organ,
people said. To play me well
demanded both hands and feet.

-gress

After a time I accepted
certain people were shy about sex
and I was one of them—at least
in English. This poem
may be sponsored
by the Society
of American Linguists.

-mogrify

If I had to be a city, I'd wish it
like Chichén Itzá, with no river
to give me away. And for water,
only the deepest clear pools—
leaping wells to the underworld.

-form

More dreams: an island given to cliffs,
a swift language I can't comprehend
except in the hush after a monsoon
when all of us appear at once, flushed
and bewildered from too much
of our own company.

-scend

If you're quiet long enough,
the whole of a life fits in a coconut
and you can whittle out the slivers
of its immaculate inner meat.

POSTCARD OF TWO BIRDS, SCATTERED FEATHERS

Here's a pre-story: a copse of sycamores,
two larks. Something on the verge

of altering. One bird
hyphens between branches, all instinct

and wing, while the other
smaller one (we'll call her she) remains

motionless, passing for tree trunk,
the ochre of bark. But the larger (our he)

has already seen her, and glides eagerly
to her bough. Their shadows merge,

a blur of wings, then separate
as swiftly—six wispy feathers

spin to the ground, the upholstery
of mercy. For a second, only the tree,

a green quiet. Then above:
two birds again in slower flight.

INTO THE ATACAMA

I

When I said I wished this trip, I meant the rush of song as we left the city. I meant the bus. I meant the woman who played her flip-flops like drumsticks against the window. For singing with strangers in a desert is like getting closer to the moon. And each moment is like the glow of the moon, caught behind clouds and then visible and then hidden again.

And when I said here, I meant elsewhere—I meant moving.

II

Out of the brush and nothing: a clutch of homes, a grove of papaya trees. For every leaning tin roof, eleven graves. And why else do people stay, if not the orchard, if not to garden around the losses that outnumber us? For what place after this much history isn't pinned to the ground with gravestones?

When I said the girl selling papaya out of her apron brought a certain movie to mind, I really meant my life—the way she tilted into the roadside, the wind blowing her skirt between her legs.

III

At dusk, more wind and a plummeting blue: the million dunes beyond us grew fainter and loomed larger. When the bus stalled, I thought: justice. Who did we think we were to cross the desert in a matter of hours?

Later, we would say it was forty years.

IV

As long as the bus moved, we knew what it was. But in stillness it could be anything, and there we were—trapped in the anything. Tumbleweed spun against rocks, into the arms of cacti, into each other, and emptiness.

We left the bus and became presidents. We became lovers and got plucky and sucked the earth dry. Thirsty, we turned back to the slower work of trust and papaya trees, the only water a hundred miles down.

V

After what might have been forty years, the bus remembered it was a bus. It hummed and carried us on—our worn shoes a thinner music against the window.

PAUSING OUTSIDE A HOUSE

Here, where a ruin longs
to be a house, and a house
to be left to ruin.

Where men blindfolded students
and pushed them down
the basement stairs.

The house almost tips
with its history, with a wish
to be simply walls

and pillars and patio—
so we could walk by, arms
loose but linked, and speak

of window trim. Here,
where a house longs
to be left a ruin,

and somebody's come to live,
to plant a trickle
of bougainvillea in the yard.

Both hungry
and over an hour late
to meet your sister, we continue.

In other houses, inhabitants
peer out at us
with the eyes of owls.

THE BARTERING

A man lifts a blue leather volume of Simone Weil from '53, brushes off a film of dirt. "Buried," the vendor says, "in a yard with those other leather ones. Two kids brought them in a wheelbarrow." The man nods—it is a common story eleven years after Pinochet: the unearthing of a book buried in fear and found in a yard or basement and sold swiftly like the furniture of the dead.

"I'll give you 500 pesos for it," he offers the vendor, the cost of an ice cream, a small box of mints.

He resists pressing the cover back, thinking of his own edition of *La Necesidad de Raices*, the night his daughter burned the book in a firepit an hour before soldiers searched the house. The moment they entered, he smelled it—the smoke still in her hair.

TIKAL

after Adam Zagajewski

I walked the forsaken city
in the rainy season

or the long light
of summer. I was obvious

or invisible, with no compass,
just this dogged pull—my kinship

with ruins. I could slip
on the wet stone steps

of Temple V
and disappear from here

as the Mayans did, or reach
the bottom again, go on to fall

from the flotsam
of some other empire.

It was dusk
or almost noon

and veins of black ants
pulsed on the fallen branches.

SECOND SNOW

If it's a natural death, you said,
let it be fast—*un ataque*

de corazón. You'd always
wanted dual passports, and to die

from anything but cancer, the castle
slowly devouring its own rooms

and walls. Every winter we return
to these questions of threshold

and dignity, whose country
is the more forgiving, as we sink

into another year of marriage.
The first walk brisk enough

to see our breath, we begin again
the discussion of endings,

then of children, as if they were the same
plaintive wish. Here, my love,

your thickest scarf, your hat.

THE DRY LANDS

Picture the fire here
like a mind in doubt.

Once it catches,
everything gives
to its silvery heat:

nests of terns, coyotes
in their dens,
great tomes of trees.

And there's no confirming
how the uncertainty begins,

no predicting
the distance it will burn.

So what to tell the person
who loves you,

the one perched
on a truck bed, tugging
at hoses?

Love can only do so much
for a blaze in the dry lands.

You want to say thanks,
what a help.

You want to say this uproar
will surely falter
at the next quarry of stones.

Knowing such fires
before, the coyotes
have already fled their dens.

THE CANDIDATE

When falsely accused
of dishonesty, a woman
may slip into a hallway
and stroke the husk of curtain
over the closest window,
the sloping musty fringe of it.

If there's no curtain,
she may stroke the glass.

If it lacks a window,
she may lean into the wall
and imagine one, crawl out of it
onto a small boat
in a covert pond.

Rowing across,
she may rub at the reproach
like a stone in her palm,
consider tossing it waterward
or let it settle in her pocket.

She may grow dishonest,
become a rambler, pants sagging
with every manner of stone.

SCENES FROM MOVING VEHICLES, II

They met at Hardy's in a highway town:
a woman and her half-grown daughters.

Took snapshots with a compact camera,
sipped milkshakes, and then the woman

was gone, part of the highway—her camera
sliding down the car roof, somersaulting

across the lanes. Hard to speak
of that sort of tumbling,

who could've left the camera there.
Why a semi sped past just then,

busting it into a hundred pieces—
film, flash, and fits of plastic, all flying

toward where the highway slopes away,
turning back to earth, aspen and undergrowth.

FROM THE SMALL BOOK OF RETURNS

I

There is my mother leaving,
my father parking, taking his time.
Somebody had to stay and belong
to these low, blue mountains.

How to know the whole
of a furtive history, quit tracing
its arc of disappointments,

which begin here — at the cut of river
where we'd come to upturn
the lighter stones, press our fingers

into the lichen, opening pockets.
So much grows on the unseen face.

II

In certain valleys of Appalachia, a translucent blue-veined berry grows, rumored to be a hallucinogen. None of us admit to having picked them, though the low-hanging clusters disappear every summer from their trees — plucked clean between late evening and dawn.

At block parties and bonfires, someone always makes a joke about the berries and their heady fragrance becomes more difficult to ignore — the strange blend of burnt sugar and slept-in sheets, of sweetness and misdemeanors.

Later, in the shadows of the trees, we lick at our fingers.

A MAÇA NO OSCURO

The story is like this: a man arrives
at the sorry farm of two sisters.

They hire him on the condition
that he sleep in the barn. A few chickens

bicker in the grass and before long
both women are in love. In my sleep,

I am the sister who slips
into that unsteady dark, finds her way

through the stink of animals,
past the bales of hay to the stranger.

Or it happens I am the one who stays
in bed, must listen to the other

crossing the yard. And I am left
with my swept room, my body

fixed in its place like a cabinet.
Either way, the intricacies of choice

are devouring. Either way, I wake
and do not recognize my life.

SEATED NUDE X

A cream tide
combs over the feet,

two breasts tilt
in their uneven way—

a faceless body
made still life, geography—

as she showed shadefall
on jimsonweed, a pelvis

the desert swept
from the heavier bones,

and a calico rose
in the socket

of a cow's skull
remembering a brown eye.

She took a life stilled
and made it shifting.

Gestures of flesh
set aside—

except for these few nudes
one X at a time

against a far rise,
a certain distance, calling.

TWO WOMEN IN A BARN

It happens that a mother becomes parchment
and rolls up gradually around the fictions
of her children. That she becomes an almond
softening in the pockets of cotton garments.
Sleeps with her glasses on in her daughter's house
and vanishes in the morning. That she's coerced
her grown child into feeding her blind horse, watching it
list oddly in the small paddock. It happens
that a daughter becomes a bottle, filling with twigs
and crinkled bits of leaves. That she likes to glint
in the water the way a glass bottle will.

A SHORT CHRONOLOGY OF ARSON

A box of matches on the patio
settles everything—by fifty, sister,
you will be master of close-up tricks,

excellent at sleight of hand. But first
you must set fire to wicker furniture
in the backyard, let the fumes

from the flaming table haze over
the rhododendrons. Seven minutes
unobserved is ample time to turn

into someone else entirely, someone
who has always been likely
but restrained, mistaken for mood.

Then the grass catches. A peppery haze
clouds the rounded back windows
of the house. Presses its way inside.

SCENES FROM MOVING VEHICLES, III

There was the rattle again
>and the tiny picture flickered

like a capped tooth
>in the mouth of the dashboard.

Your door, her mother said.
>Meaning *open it,* the daughter thought,

meaning *fix it.* Didn't think
>of how they were moving,

the two of them, and the highway
>was not—that the outside world

would snatch her so readily,
>become the trunk of an elephant

and pluck her from her seat,
>lifting her toward its bizarre, gray

immensity. But her mother
>was quicker than the world

and held her back;
>how to hold onto that.

MADDOX ROAD

Shucking corn on the veranda, my sister said
she didn't care that her father had dropped by
or that I'd finally met him. Later, I found her
outside again, staring at the fallow fields and shadows
around our mother's rented house, the row
of weathered tobacco shacks along one edge, saddled
with their years of emptiness and disuse, and she said
this had all been plantation land, that her father's family
had worked here. He'd told her so once coming down
this road and she had a feeling if she stayed here
long enough, something of meaning, of consolation
might make itself clear. And because we're not close,
I asked if I could sit with her and we listened
to the pickups shudder past, invisible after nightfall,
and between them the call of an owl—the wind bearing
strands of corn silk we'd missed into the unseen.

SLOW TRAIN

When the station appears,
stairwell cleared of snow.

When arriving in a glycerin light,
the platform salted and tended

like a fish. When I glimpse
my mother there

and she becomes the stairwell.
When between us things

have rubbed thin and breakable
like a sliver of soap.

When years like stairwells.
When cleared of snow.

IV

NOCTURNE WITH WAKING BEAR

By twilight, the accepted empire
had spent itself and gone.

One brown bear remained.

Exhausted, we sat and watched her.
The sweep of her paw.

How she ripped at our colossal
bags of garbage like so many gifts.

Our one and lovely bear, I said.

But really, she belonged to no one,
as we are no one's.

Around my neck hung a white sling
with a child in it.

I didn't know how long
she'd been slumbering there.

SCENES FROM MOVING VEHICLES, IV

Someone's stolen the headlights,
wrenched the metal back like eyelids.

Bewildered, a girl and her father
show the holes to the police where
their lights had been, wires exposed
and crimped into question marks.

The girl wonders if her father, too,
is thinking: *why our car, why blindness?*

And, when they drive on,
if the same fuzzy under-scene
of her mother persists for him,
if, at every strangeness,
he is also brought back to her.

The sun sinks, its pink rim
dims tangerine—storied light,
where the reckoning comes in.

THE FUTURE

I hear the sheep that move across it,
the silver click of their split hooves.

I hear the bells around their necks
and the dull clanks in the swell.

For they are always there,
a certain number of broken bells.

AT SOME POINT AFTER WE SEALED
THE WINDOWS

We started to mispronounce
our consonants, then the vowels,

till our names for one another
turned slippery as marbles, clacking

against teeth. Gradually
we stopped calling out

to each other in the dark,
and doubts rose cold; river water

after the thaw. Were the windows locked?
How was it we stopped thought

long enough to sleep before?
As no one could address them,

the smaller children came to forget
who they belonged to, wandered far

into the rubble, and we fed
whoever entered the kitchen

muddy-eyed and ravenous.
Unnamed, there was nothing

they would not eat. When even
the cauliflower dwindled, we pickled

what remained, and saved it
for ourselves. The break:

a quiet like a lid, months
of this, and our tongues

began fixing upon new sounds,
pinning them to objects

and to our skin where it flinched.
We've started now to whisper,

strangers still. To settle
on meanings, to speak again.

THE END OF AUGUSTO

Within an hour, people are burning tires in alleyways,
others deciding which calla lilies, which prayers

for his funeral. Back in New York, the two of us
linger over French toast and a picked-over bowl

of red grapes; outside, the keen wail of an ambulance.
This is what the end of an era is like:

this quiet inside—and out—a siren passing,
its sound filling our ready mouths.

LANDSCAPE WITH IRONY

When the water
recedes this far,
I start across
to the continent,
my belongings
in a wheelbarrow.
Over the sand,
over the bones
of pirates
clattering like plates.
My stride grows long
and willful,
only to stop
at this sudden octopus,
washed-up
and gull-pecked,
its severed tentacles
in their delicate desire
to be drawn
impossibly back
to the body
and refastened.

PAINTED GOURD HUNG FROM AN OPEN GATE

My hollowed,
my bell of a vegetable turned drum.

My better eye
in exits, my sexed-up from and to.

My everything
as symbol, though probably of nothing new.

My find,
my glorified, my might-as-well, and did.

ABOUT A FIELD

After the last house,
              the land extends
              like a hand before the mouth of a horse.

You come to it all year,
              in high drifts of snow,
              in stands of new grass
              and joe-pye weed.

                      You walk through five-foot asters,
and understand *momentary*.
              You understand *beauty*.

You turn seven. Your family is a knotted button
and it unfastens.

              In the world beyond,
                    a war begins.

You pay attention,
recognize now
some of the dimensions of loss.

              You want to offer up something,
              but to whom,
                  to what?

You move and move.
Take on another hemisphere, try to grasp
what happens between one country
and another.
End up married.

You understand *become*.
You understand *compromise*.

You turn quieter.
A salty coastal wind
carries pollen from a cluster of asters
into your open hand.

For a second, you are everywhere
you have ever been.

HIGHWAY TOWN

All along, all our lives, it was closing time:
a coat of dark birds fastening over the sky.

Think of how we said *See you,* but meant *enough,
good night.* Think of all the roads coned off

like scenes of a crime, the ramps delivering
our aunts and uncles to a place where

they would knock and knock, and no one
would answer. What's next, one of them would say,

and pull the stubborn door down
over our loveliest garage. But it would never close,

not completely—a seam of light sneaking in
between the lowered door and the ground.

Half our town was conceived
in that cavernous garage, on a scrap

of carpet or the gritty floor, backs arching
in the partial light of that floating door.

TO BYZANTIUM, BY TRAIN

Assume a window seat and wait
for the woman with the long-tailed birds
who will wake you. As you travel,

she will gradually become your age,
after which someone else
will enter your car, an optimist

who will make you more agnostic
than you ever suspected—the smell
of pheasants suddenly impossible.

Slip off your sandals. You may need
to unbutton your sleeves, or admit
the weakness that is your art.

Take refuge in the window:
the inarguable grace of a farm
just past, or passing, or to come.

Then a shift in landscape—
something hung on a stick,
the scalped skin of a goat,

or a coat too tattered
for any weather. Whatever it is,
know that you have come to love

the thrum of this train
and the woman who woke you
with her crate of birds.

To love even the optimist
and beyond him
that strange, draped pelt.

NOTES

The arena described in "The Wailers in Estadio Nacional" refers to the national soccer stadium in Santiago, Chile where detainees were held and tortured after Augusto Pinochet's military coup on September 11th, 1973. Many of the detainees remain missing.

"Pausing Outside a House" borrows its first line and a half from Yehuda Amichai's poem "In the mountains of Jerusalem" as it appears in Glenda Abramson and Tudor Parfitt's translation published in *The Great Tranquility* (The Sheep Meadow Press, 1997).

"Tikal" is after Adam Zagajewski's poem, "I Walked Through the Medieval Town," as translated by Clare Cavenaugh in *From Mysticism to Beginners* (Farrar, Straus, and Giroux, 1997).

"A *Maça No Oscuro*" is based on a novel by Brazilian writer Clarice Lispector. The English title is "The Apple in the Dark."

RECENT TITLES FROM ALICE JAMES BOOKS

ALICE JAMES BOOKS has been publishing exclusively poetry since 1973. One of the few presses in the country that is run collectively, the cooperative selects manuscripts for publication through both regional and national annual competitions. New regional authors become active members of the cooperative, participating in the editorial decisions of the press. The press, which historically has placed an emphasis on publishing women poets, was named for Alice James, sister of William and Henry, whose fine journal and gift for writing went unrecognized within her lifetime.

TYPESET AND DESIGNED BY
DEDE CUMMINGS AND CAROLYN KASPER / DCDESIGN
PRINTED BY THOMSON-SHORE
ON 50% POSTCONSUMER RECYCLED PAPER
PROCESSED CHLORINE-FREE